2-cent Haiku

Alexander Silva

BookLeaf Publishing

Presentation by *BookLeaf Publishing*

Web: www.bookleafpub.com

E-mail: info@bookleafpub.com

ISBN: 9789357744003

First edition 2023

For my late friend Jon

There is help available

It's never too late

afsp.org

PREFACE

There's nothing deep here
Sometimes things are just simple
Don't let it be you

Wise words are easy
Action and change, not so much
Haikus are easy

Feelings can be hard
Dire, urgent, and silly
Here they are, exposed

Things don't get better
You get better at the things
One day at a time

Advice is the worst
Something something, get back up
Something, try again

Perfectionists!
I'd like to report a crime
- an illegal haiku

Building character
Thanks for all the life lessons
No more please, all grown

"Hope it's a good day"
Let's not hold ourselves hostage
Glide through the bad ones

Nothing to see here
The next one's pretty good though
(Please skip this haiku)

Oof, expectations
This is great, but not that great
Oof, disappointment

I'm in charge of me!
I just wish others saw it
I'd feel so happy

Being right is key
Here lies the victor, alone
She sure had good points

It's not Me v. You
It's Us v. The Problem
No winners, no score

Expectations met
Nobody's disappointed
Success tastes so bland

Want to make mom proud?

It's done with one simple trick

Be proud of **urself**

Jokes on you, suckers!
You knew this stuff already!
Sorry, no refunds

Just like the last time
Please know you'll get through this too
That one simple trick

All joking aside
You know what you need to do
Please put down this book

It's never goodbye
This is just "see you later"
In spirit, at best

www.ingramcontent.com/pod-product-compliance
Lightning Source LLC
La Vergne TN
LVHW010904200726
843508LV00012B/2980